The British Museum

SECRET TREASURES OF ANCIENT EGYPT

Kate Sparrow • Esther Aarts

This publication accompanies the BP exhibition
Sunken cities: Egypt's lost worlds at the British Museum
from 19 May to 27 November 2016, organised with the
Hilti Foundation and the Institut Européen d'Archéologie
Sous-Marine, in collaboration with the Ministry of
Antiquities of the Arab Republic of Egypt.

London Borough of Enfield	
91200000595826	
Askews & Holts	Mar-2017
JUNIOR NON-FICT	£11.99

First published 2016 by Nosy Crow Ltd
The Crow's Nest, 10a Lant Street
London SE1 1QR
www.nosycrow.com

ISBN 978 0 85763 795 6 (HB)
ISBN 978 0 85763 757 4 (PB)

Nosy Crow and associated logos are trademarks
and/or registered trademarks of Nosy Crow Ltd.

Text © Kate Sparrow 2016
Illustrations © Esther Aarts 2016

The right of Kate Sparrow to be identified as the author
and Esther Aarts to be identified as the illustrator of this work has been asserted.

All rights reserved.

This book is sold subject to the condition that it shall not,
by way of trade or otherwise, be lent, hired out or otherwise circulated in
any form of binding or cover other than that in which it is published.
No part of this publication may be reproduced, stored in a retrieval system,
or transmitted in any form or by any means
(electronic, mechanical, photocopying, recording or otherwise)
without the prior written permission of Nosy Crow Ltd.

A CIP catalogue record for this book is available from the British Library.

Printed in Spain.
Papers used by Nosy Crow are made from wood
grown in sustainable forests.

1 3 5 7 9 8 6 4 2 (HB)
1 3 5 7 9 8 6 4 2 (PB)

CONTENTS

- INTRODUCTION — pages 4–5
- LOST... AND FOUND! — pages 6–7
- TREASURE TROVE — pages 8–9
- WATER WORLD — pages 10–11
- IT'S ALL GREEK TO ME! — pages 12–13
- SHARE AND SHARE ALIKE — pages 14–15
- FRIENDS AND FAMILY — pages 16–17
- MIX-AND-MATCH GODS — pages 18–19
- "MY DADDY IS A MUMMY!" — pages 20–21
- LUCKY OR YUCKY? — pages 22–23
- PARTY TIME! — pages 24–25
- DISASTER! — pages 26–27
- RESCUING THE PAST — pages 28–29
- INDEX AND ACKNOWLEDGEMENTS — Pages 30–32
- PLUS FOLD-OUT MAP AND TIMELINE!

Under the waters of Abukir Bay, Egypt, beneath layers of sand and clay, lie the ruins of two great, ancient cities.

These are the legendary lost worlds of Egypt: the ancient cities of Canopus and Thonis-Heracleion.

Just over a thousand years ago, catastrophe struck and the cities sank under the sea.

Time passed, and the cities were lost.

Until now…

LOST... AND FOUND!

IMAGINE A BAY, BUSY WITH BOATS. Imagine that far beneath the waters lie two entire ancient cities, hidden from view. Ships pass over them every day, yet nobody notices the ruins on the seabed below...

Imagine a very big triangular area of water. Each side is 10 kilometres long — that's as long as 100 football pitches! It would take the average person 6 hours to walk around the edge of this triangle.

WIDE SCAN SONAR

KEY WORDS

SONAR directs pulses of sound at an object and uses the echo that bounces off it to find the object.

NMR detects differences in the Earth's magnetic field created by buried objects.

An **ARCHAEOLOGIST** is a person who finds and studies objects from past and present civilisations.

THE HISTORY OF THE MYSTERY

Scholars and experts had searched for the lost cities for a very long time — but nobody had found them underneath the dark, murky water, full of sand and silt from the River Nile. The cities and the objects in them were covered in algae and mud, and hidden from sight.

In 1933, Captain Cull of the Royal Air Force noticed something in the bay as he flew over in his plane. Prince Omar Toussoun of Egypt then explored the area, and found stone columns and sculptures!

NUCLEAR MAGNETIC RESONANCE (NMR)

MEET FRANCK

NEEDLE IN A HAYSTACK

Then, in 1996, the underwater archaeologist Franck Goddio brought a team into Abukir Bay. The team used sonar to create maps of the seabed. The maps told them exactly where the lost cities might be found. And so they began to sift down through metres of sand and clay, to reveal the sunken treasures…

Underwater archaeologists have to be good at finding things… and great at swimming!

TREASURE TROVE

FRANCK GODDIO AND HIS TEAM HAD DISCOVERED THE LOST CITIES!

After years of careful work, in the year 2000, they unearthed incredible treasures from the past. So far, they have uncovered hundreds of beautiful objects from the lost worlds of Canopus and Thonis-Heracleion.

Here are some of the treasures they have found...

UNDERWATER EVIDENCE

BELL

LEAD BARGE

PERFUME BOTTLE

Which is your favourite treasure?

OSIRIS-CANOPUS JAR

GOLD COIN

SPHINX STATUE

PHARAOH STATUE

STELE SHOWING THE DECREE OF SAIS

IBIS SARCOPHAGI

GOLDEN-EYED OSIRIS

Objects are not to scale — many are so big, it would take thousands of pages to fit them all in!

GOLD DISH

HEAD OF PHARAOH NECTANEBO II

GOLD EARRING

SPHINX INCENSE BURNER

SERAPIS HEAD

THE HAPY-NESS SCALE

This amazing statue of the Egyptian god Hapy is as tall as a tall giraffe! He is taller than two tall men and much, much, MUCH taller than you!

A giraffe

Two tall men

You

HE'S A HEFTY HAPY TOO... HE WEIGHS 4.5 TONNES — ABOUT AS MUCH AS AN AFRICAN ELEPHANT!

WATER WORLD

THANKS TO THESE BRAVE, CLEVER UNDERWATER EXPLORERS, WE CAN NOW UNDERSTAND HOW THE TWO LOST CITIES WOULD HAVE LOOKED.

At the edge of ancient Egypt, where the River Nile met the sea, stood two busy seaports, Canopus and Thonis-Heracleion. It was a watery world, a land of lakes and marshes dotted with islands and sandbanks. A big, wide canal connected the two cities. Boats loaded with cargo came and went through the ports.

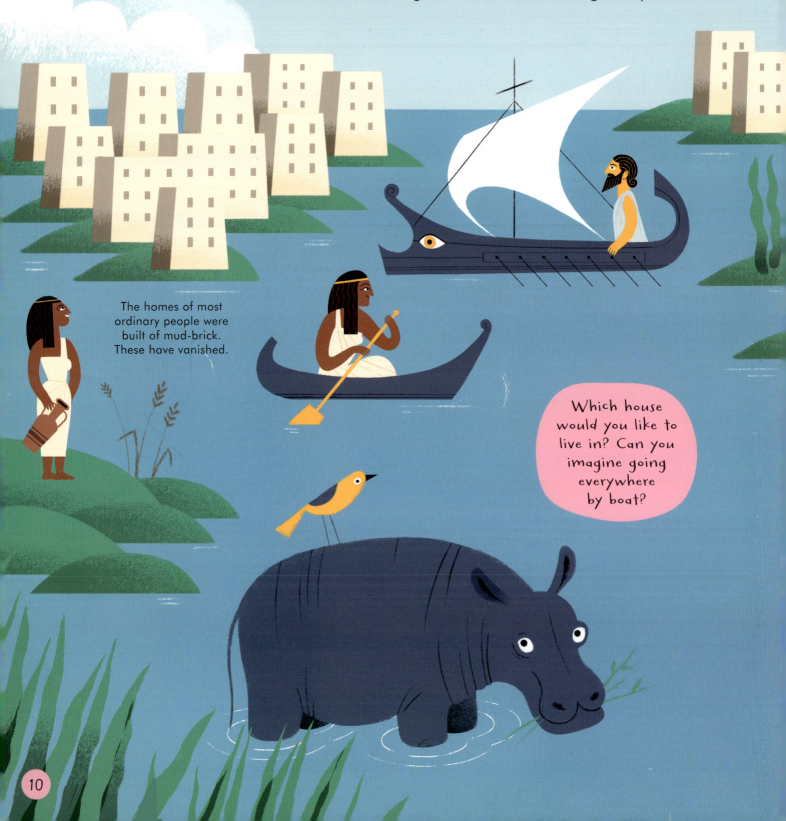

The homes of most ordinary people were built of mud-brick. These have vanished.

Which house would you like to live in? Can you imagine going everywhere by boat?

ANCIENT GREEK ALPHABET

Αα Alpha	Ββ Beta
Γγ Gamma	Δδ Delta
Εε Epsilon	Ζζ Zeta
Ηη Eta	Θθ Theta
Ιι Iota	Κκ Kappa
Λλ Lambda	Μμ Mu
Νν Nu	Ξξ Xi
Οο Omicron	Ππ Pi
Ρρ Rho	Σσς Sigma
Ττ Tau	Υυ Upsilon
Φφ Phi	Χχ Chi
Ψψ Psi	Ωω Omega

IT'S ALL GREEK TO ME!

VISITORS FROM GREECE WERE THE FIRST 'TOURISTS' TO EGYPT. Canopus and Thonis-Heracleion would have been the first cities they saw as they arrived. Those Greeks certainly made their mark!

Greek graffiti at an Egyptian temple at Abu-Simbel.

Imagine arriving in a new place, where you did not speak the language! The Greeks and Egyptians had to find a way to understand one another.

GREEKS

Try having a conversation using only sign language!

EGYPTIANS

"ANCIENT EGYPTIAN WRITING IS CALLED HIEROGLYPHICS AND CAN BE READ IN EITHER DIRECTION — UP OR DOWN, RIGHT TO LEFT OR LEFT TO RIGHT."

ANCIENT EGYPTIAN HIEROGLYPHS

The Rosetta Stone is carved with words in Egyptian and in Greek. It became the key to deciphering the ancient Egyptian language. It tells us that the Greeks and Egyptians understood one another… eventually.

Try writing your name using these two ancient alphabets. Can you spot the missing letters?

ANCIENT GREEK SCRIPT

EGYPTIAN HIEROGLYPHIC ALPHABET

A B C D E F G H I J K L M N O P Q R S T U V W X Y Z

The cities of Canopus and Thonis-Heracleion were well known in the ancient world, and the Egyptian city of Thonis-Heracleion was even named by the Greeks after one of their gods, Herakles.

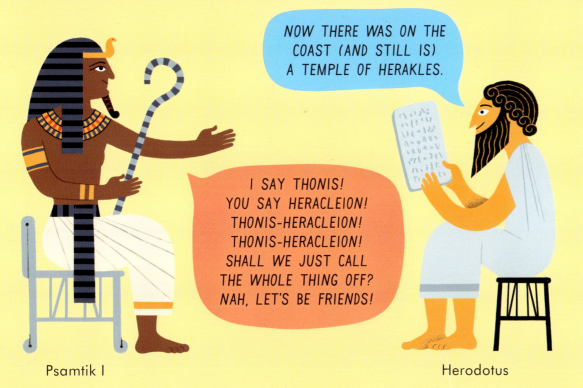

"NOW THERE WAS ON THE COAST (AND STILL IS) A TEMPLE OF HERAKLES."

"I SAY THONIS! YOU SAY HERACLEION! THONIS-HERACLEION! THONIS-HERACLEION! SHALL WE JUST CALL THE WHOLE THING OFF? NAH, LET'S BE FRIENDS!"

Psamtik I

Herodotus

SHARE AND SHARE ALIKE

THE ANCIENT GREEKS OFTEN SAILED ACROSS THE MEDITERRANEAN SEA, TO TRADE WITH THEIR EGYPTIAN NEIGHBOURS.

The two peoples had known each other for hundreds of years. Like many neighbours, they did not always understand each other, but they became friends.

Greek aristocrats, poets and thinkers came to Egypt to share ideas, and to see Egypt's wonders for themselves. Others came to make their fortune by trading with the Egyptians.

The Egyptians were amazed by the Greek people who came from across the sea, wearing stunning bronze armour. Some even named the Mediterranean the 'Sea of Greeks'. And the ancient Greeks thought of Egypt as a fascinating place, full of wonders and treasures.

The Greeks brought their language to Egypt… and so much more!

These Greek coins, or tetradrachms, were made in Athens, and found in Egypt.

UNDERWATER EVIDENCE

This helmet was worn by a Greek soldier who may have fought for the Egyptian army.

This tiny perfume bottle would fit in the palm of your hand! It was made in Athens, and found at Thonis-Heracleion.

KEY WORDS

A **PHARAOH** is an ancient Egyptian ruler.

TAX is money that must be paid to the government.

An **IMPORT** comes into one country from another.

An **EXPORT** is sent out of one country to another.

PAPYRUS is a plant that grew by the River Nile and was used to make things like paper, shoes and rope.

Even though they were friends, the pharaohs still demanded that all Greek traders paid them taxes.

Greek goods were traded to Egypt (imports) and Egyptian goods were sent back to Greece (exports).

The Greeks took Egyptian grains, papyrus, and alum and natron (used for fabric dying) back home on their ships. They valued Egyptian perfume, scarabs and amulets.

As well as Greek amphorae and pottery, Egyptians wanted Greek silver, copper and lead.

Have you ever bought something from another country?

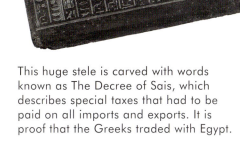

This huge stele is carved with words known as The Decree of Sais, which describes special taxes that had to be paid on all imports and exports. It is proof that the Greeks traded with Egypt.

THE SUNKEN SPHINXES: SHARING ART AND STORIES

Two sphinxes were found close to each other under water. They have Hellenistic faces — this means they have links with both Egypt and Greece. One of their heads was probably a portrait of Cleopatra's father.

Cleopatra VII was a great queen of ancient Egypt, and one of the most fascinating women of all time.

A **SCARAB** is a beetle. Amulets were made in the shape of scarabs.

An **AMULET** is an object, often an ornament, believed to protect its owner.

An **AMPHORA** is a tall jug used to store wine and oil.

A **STELE** is a tall, decorated, inscribed slab made from wood or stone.

A **SPHINX** is a mythical creature. In ancient Egypt, it had a human head and the body of a lion.

FRIENDS AND FAMILY

RELIGION WAS VERY IMPORTANT IN THE LIVES OF ANCIENT EGYPTIANS AND GREEKS.

Just as it is for many people today, a person's religion was part of his or her identity. The Egyptian pharaohs were wise enough to let the Greeks build temples to their own gods.

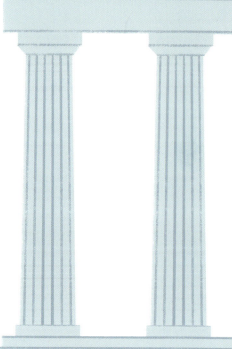

The Greeks brought gifts with them, to offer to the gods. They asked the gods for divine protection for dangerous sea journeys, and they asked for success in their business deals.

It must have felt strange at times for the Greeks, to find themselves in a foreign land, so far from home. Their sanctuaries were safe places, where they could meet and socialise, and share their religious rituals with new friends.

KEY WORDS

RELIGION is the belief in a god or a group of gods.

IDENTITY means the beliefs and qualities that make someone who they are.

A RITUAL is a special ceremony always done in the same way each time.

ALEXANDER THE GREAT was a Greek king, who also became pharaoh of Egypt, and emperor of Persia and Asia. He was one of the greatest conquerors of all time.

Greek traders, soldiers and sailors were welcomed in Egypt, and many decided to stay. Many Greeks married Egyptian women.

SHARING GODS HELPS US FEEL CLOSER!

Naturally, mixed families wanted to share each other's customs. The two peoples came to recognise similarities between many of their gods. Sharing gods was a way of belonging.

What are the important parts of your identity?

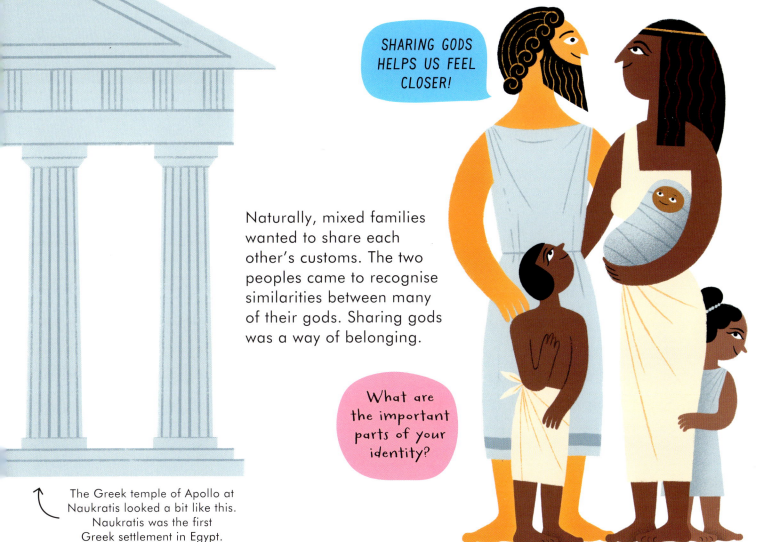

The Greek temple of Apollo at Naukratis looked a bit like this. Naukratis was the first Greek settlement in Egypt.

ALEXANDER'S GREAT IDEA!

One of the most important Greeks to arrive in Egypt was Alexander the Great.

Alexander's great idea was to say that he was descended from a mixture of both Greek and Egyptian gods, making him a worthy ruler to both peoples. He also asked both Greeks and Egyptians to help him rule, which made him very popular with everyone.

EGYPTIAN GOD AMUN

GREEK GOD ZEUS

MIX-AND-MATCH GODS

GREEKS AND EGYPTIANS REALISED THAT MANY OF THEIR GODS WERE SIMILAR.

Ancient art tells us what some of the gods might have looked like, but others we can only imagine…

Which of the ancient Greek and Egyptian gods are your favourites and why?

- I'M KING OF THE GODS!
- HEY, ME TOO! WATCH ME THROW THIS THING!
- YOU'RE LIKE ME…
- …AND I'M LIKE YOU!
- BUT I LIKE POINTY HATS!
- ROMANTIC CRISIS? CALL ISIS!

Amun — Zeus — Osiris — Dionysos — Isis

KEY GODS

AMUN was the king of ancient Egyptian gods.

ZEUS was the most important of all the ancient Greek gods. He was similar to the Egyptian god Amun.

OSIRIS was the Egyptian god of the underworld, regeneration and rebirth.

DIONYSOS was the Greek god of wine and celebration. Greeks and Egyptians believed he was similar to Osiris.

ISIS was the Egyptian goddess of magic. She was the wife of Osiris.

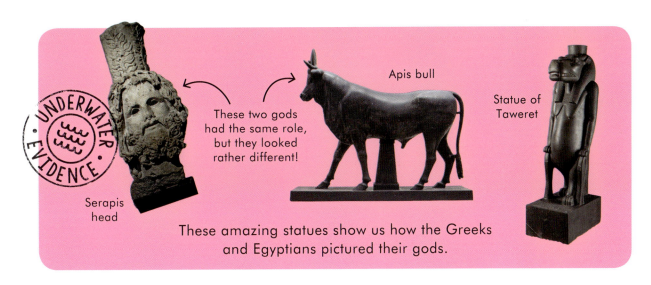

These two gods had the same role, but they looked rather different!

UNDERWATER EVIDENCE

Serapis head

Apis bull

Statue of Taweret

These amazing statues show us how the Greeks and Egyptians pictured their gods.

Aphrodite	Taweret	Hapy	Apis	Serapis
APHRODITE was the Greek goddess of love and beauty. The Greeks believed she was like Isis.	**TAWERET** was the Egyptian divine guardian of pregnancy and childhood. She was known as the 'Great One'.	**HAPY** was the Egyptian god of the River Nile's flood.	**APIS** was a sacred bull. He could predict the future.	**SERAPIS** was a new god, created for the Greeks. He was similar to the Egyptian gods, Osiris and Apis.

"MY DADDY IS A MUMMY!"

ACCORDING TO THE EGYPTIANS, OSIRIS WAS THE FIRST KING OF EARTH.

When he was king, he taught people agriculture and gave them laws and peace.

But then his evil brother Seth murdered him. He drowned him and then he cut up Osiris's body and scattered the pieces all around Egypt!

Osiris's wife Isis was a great magician. She found every piece of Osiris's body and put him back together.

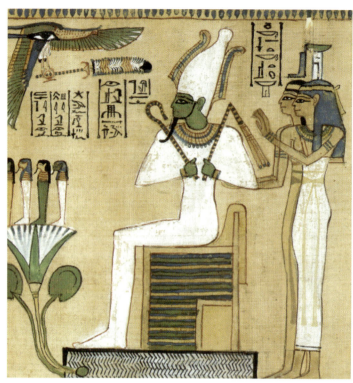

Osiris is shown here with green skin!

I AM OSIRIS, THE FIRST MUMMY.

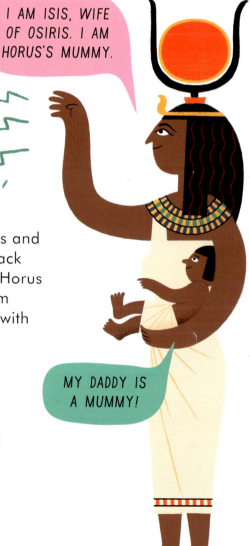

I AM ISIS, WIFE OF OSIRIS. I AM HORUS'S MUMMY.

After rebuilding his body, Isis and other gods brought Osiris back to life. Soon after, their son Horus was born. Isis hid Horus from his enemies, protecting him with powerful magic.

MY DADDY IS A MUMMY!

Would you like to live forever? What would you do with your time if you were immortal?

IF WE TALK ABOUT SOMEONE WHO HAS DIED, WE PUT 'OSIRIS' IN FRONT OF THEIR NAME.

LIKE OSIRIS-GREAT-GRANDAD!

WHEN SOMEONE DIES, WE COPY WHAT THE GODS DID FOR OSIRIS WHEN THEY MADE HIM INTO THE FIRST MUMMY — WE MUMMIFY OUR DEAD TO HELP THEM IN THE AFTERLIFE.

KEY WORDS

A **MUMMY** is a dead body which has been embalmed, or preserved, before burial, using special salt and cloth wrappings.

IMMORTAL means something that lives forever.

The **AFTERLIFE** is the place where some people believe they will go after they die.

A **MYTH** is an ancient story that explains how or why something happens.

These underwater discoveries show how important the myth and worship of Osiris were in ancient Egypt.

Golden-eyed Osiris statue.

UNDERWATER EVIDENCE

This garden vat was filled with a soil-and-barley figure of Osiris and sprayed with water eight days in a row, until it germinated during the annual Mysteries of Osiris festival.

An Osiris-Canopus amulet was thought to protect the owner from danger.

This beautiful statue shows an Egyptian queen as the goddess Isis.

21

LUCKY OR YUCKY?

THE EGYPTIANS AND GREEKS AGREED ON MANY THINGS, BUT THERE WAS ONE IMPORTANT THING THEY DID NOT AGREE ABOUT... ANIMAL MUMMIES!

Some animals, like bulls, were seen by the Egyptians as the living form of a god. When they died, they were carefully mummified, buried in expensive boxes called sarcophagi... and then worshipped!

Other animal mummies were offerings to the gods that looked like them. And some animals were mummified to be messengers between people and gods.

As part of their worship of animals they considered sacred, Egyptians made and buried mummies of bulls, ibises, hawks, dogs and cats. They buried each species in its own separate cemetery.

The cat goddess Bastet.

Some cat mummies were offerings to Bastet.

WE EGYPTIANS SAY THAT SOME ANIMALS ARE SACRED. THEY ARE THE LIVING FORM OF A GOD.

WE GREEKS THINK THE EGYPTIAN TREND OF ANIMAL WORSHIP IS VERY STRANGE. AN ANIMAL CANNOT BE A GOD!

Are some animals important to you? Would you want to mummify them?

In animal cemeteries, millions of mummies have been discovered! Some mummies were mixed-up: they had parts of different animals and even human bits in them!

HOW TO MAKE AN ANIMAL MUMMY

1. TAKE OUT DEAD ANIMAL'S BRAIN, HEART, LUNGS AND GUTS
2. DRY THE ANIMAL'S BODY WITH SALT
3. APPLY SACRED OILS INSIDE AND OUT
4. WRAP IN BANDAGES
5. BURY THE MUMMY

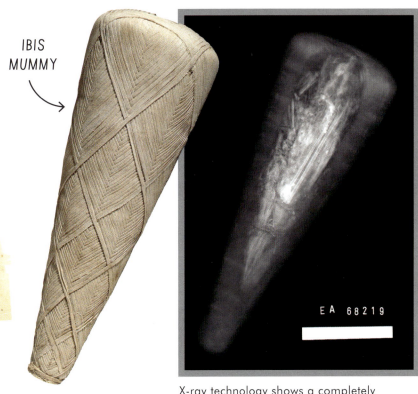

IBIS MUMMY

X-ray technology shows a completely preserved ibis bird inside this carefully wrapped mummy.

KEY WORDS

BASTET was an Egyptian goddess who often took the form of a cat.

SACRED means something that is very special and connected with a god.

A SARCOPHAGUS is a stone coffin that held a dead body, human or animal.

An IBIS is a bird that the ancient Egyptians believed was sacred.

PARTY TIME!

DESPITE THEIR DIFFERENCES, GREEKS AND EGYPTIANS LIVED HAPPILY TOGETHER.

Sharing beliefs and celebrating festivals together helped the Greeks and Egyptians feel closer. One of the most exciting times of the year in Egypt was the festival of the Mysteries of Osiris. The Greeks celebrated it too, because Osiris reminded them of their own god, Dionysos.

Lamps lit up the canal at night, and were also used in some sacred ceremonies.

These little lead barges were thrown into the canal as votive objects to please the gods.

Ladles like this, called simpula, were used when making sacred figures of Osiris and also to pour special drinks for the gods.

This festival was the most important religious celebration in ancient Egypt, and it lasted for 18 days of the month of Khoiak, which was in the autumn. Egyptians and Greeks travelled to join the celebrations by canal and waterway. The Grand Canal linking the cities of Canopus and Thonis-Heracleion had a sacred purpose during the Mysteries: on the 29th Khoiak, figures of Osiris were carried in procession along the Grand Canal, on a barge.

What do you think it felt like during Khoiak? Have you ever been to a festival?

"DAY AND NIGHT, THERE ARE CROWDS OF MEN AND WOMEN IN BOATS, SINGING AND DANCING"

— Strabo, an ancient Greek historian

The sistrum was an ancient percussion instrument that made a loud rattling sound. Objects like this have been found under water.

All along the ancient procession route, offerings and votive objects have been found, which were special gifts for the gods. People did not want their offerings for the gods to be found and used again, so they sometimes broke their gifts before they dropped them into the canal!

As well as Egyptian votive objects, ritual objects connected to the Greek god Dionysos have been found. This shows that Greeks also took part in the Mysteries of Osiris, adapting the rituals so that they could celebrate in their own way.

KEY WORDS

A **FESTIVAL** is a special time of celebration.

KHOIAK is the fourth month of the Egyptian year, from mid-October to mid-November. It was linked with the end of the flooding of the Nile.

A **BARGE** is a long, narrow boat specially designed to fit in a canal.

A **VOTIVE OBJECT** was used to honour or thank a god.

DISASTER!

THE TWO AMAZING CITIES OF CANOPUS AND THONIS-HERACLEION WERE EVENTUALLY LOST IN TIME... How could two such busy, vibrant cities simply sink beneath the waves? How could a place so alive with celebration and beauty just vanish?

Archaeologists believe that many different things caused the cities to disappear. There were earthquakes...

tsunamis...

rising sea levels…

And, finally, the heavy weight of the massive stone buildings made them slowly sink down, down, down… Until they became buried on the seabed.

> Have you ever felt your feet sink into wet sand, just like the sinking cities?

RESCUING THE PAST

LUCKILY THESE TREASURES FROM THE PAST ARE NO LONGER LOST!

Franck Goddio and his team have uncovered many amazing treasures, but there is more work to do. Now that they have surveyed and explored the underwater site, the divers know where to look. It's time to go into the water!

PRINCESS DUDA

The water is ten metres deep. This is actually fairly shallow water, so the team can use normal scuba-diving equipment. They have enough air in their tanks to work in two-hour shifts.

They use UV torches to help them see, and special underwater notebooks to make very important notes.

BAG 'EM AND TAG 'EM!

I need a wee!

10m

TEN METRES IS AS HIGH AS A TWO-STOREY HOUSE!

This 11-metre-long barge is still under the sea. It's one of 69 ships found so far at Thonis-Heracleion, the largest number of ancient boats ever discovered!

2m

The deep mud and clay have preserved the treasures, so that even after hundreds and hundreds of years, they are still intact – and so beautiful!

The archaeologists live and work on their boat, the Princess Duda.

Heavier objects are carefully lifted to the surface by a special crane.

FINDS OF THE FUTURE?

The rediscovery of the two lost cities is uniquely important. By studying the ruins and their treasures, we are learning more than ever before about the relationship between ancient Egypt and the Greek world.

SO FAR, THE TEAM HAVE EXCAVATED LESS THAN 5% OF THE VAST SUBMERGED SITE...

That means there is 95% left to explore! Hundreds of sunken treasures have been found... What other treasures might still be hidden?

Will you become the next underwater explorer?

All photos, unless otherwise stated, are by Christoph Gerigk © Franck Goddio/ Hilti Foundation

Cover and title page:

Head of a pharaoh
Canopus
3rd century BC

Pages 4–5:

Various sunken treasures at Canopus

Pages 6–7:

Franck Goddio

Pages 8–9:

Votive boat
Thonis-Heracleion
4th century BC

Cypriot gold coin
Thonis-Heracleion
355-353 BC

Osiris-Canopus jar
Canopus
1st–2nd century AD

Sphinx
Thonis-Heracleion
4th century BC

INDEX

Decree of Sais,
Stele of Thonis-Heracleion
Thonis-Heracleion
380 BC

Small sarcophagi for animal mummies
Thonis-Heracleion
664–525 BC

Pharaoh with khepresh crown
Thonis-Heracleion
664–380 BC

Earring with the head of a mythical animal
Thonis-Heracleion
4th–2nd century BC

Bell
Thonis-Heracleion
6th–2nd century BC

Gold dish
Thonis-Heracleion
4th–2nd century BC

Statuette of Osiris
Thonis-Heracleion
664–332 BC

Head of Nectanebo II
Canopus
360–342 BC

Cypriot incense burner
Thonis-Heracleion
Early 5th century BC

Colossal statue of Hapy
Thonis-Heracleion
4th or 3rd century BC

Head of Serapis
Canopus
2nd century BC

Pages 12–13:

Greek graffiti on Egyptian temple
Photo: Ross Thomas, on behalf of the Naukratis Project © The Trustees of the British Museum
Abu-Simbel, Egypt
Graffiti dated 593 BC

Rosetta Stone
Photo © The Trustees of the British Museum
Rashid (Rosetta), Egypt
196 BC

Pages 14–15:

Tetradrachms (Greek coins)
Photo © The Trustees of the British Museum
Found in Naukratis; from Athens
450–406 BC

Greek helmet
Thonis-Heracleion
5th–4th century BC

Athenian perfume bottle
Thonis-Heracleion
c 410–400 BC

Sphinx
Alexandria
1st century BC

Cleopatra seated on a barge (detail)
After Sir Lawrence Alma-Tadema,
The Meeting of Antony and Cleopatra
Photo © The Trustees of the British Museum
1883

Scarab amulet
Photo © The Trustees of the British Museum
Naukratis
600–570 BC

Amphora
Photo © The Trustees of the British Museum
Tell Dafana, Egypt
c 550–500 BC

Pages 16–17:

Statue of Zeus
Photo © The Trustees of the British Museum
Hungary
1st–2nd century AD

Figure of Amun-Ra
Photo © The Trustees of the British Museum
Egypt
332–30 BC

Alexander the Great
Photo © The Trustees of the British Museum
Alexandria
2nd–1st century BC

Pages 18–19:

Statue of Taweret
Karnak, Egypt
664–610 BC

Apis bull
Alexandria
AD 117–138

Pages 20–21:

Papyrus of Hunefer
Photo © The Trustees of the British Museum
Thebes, Egypt
1285 BC

Osiris-Canopus amulet
Canopus
30 BC–AD 395

Garden vat
Thonis-Heracleion
4th–2nd century BC

A queen (possibly Cleopatra III) dressed as Isis
Thonis-Heracleion
2nd century BC

Pages 22–23:

Bastet statue
Photo © The Trustees of the British Museum
Bubastis, Egypt
900 BC–600 BC

Cat mummy
Photo © The Trustees of the British Museum
Abydos, Egypt
Roman Period, perhaps 1st century AD

Ibis mummy
Photo © The Trustees of the British Museum
Saqqara, Egypt
332–30 BC

Pages 24–25:

Egyptian oil lamp
Thonis-Heracleion
3rd century BC

Wheel-made oil lamp
Thonis-Heracleion
End of 4th–3rd century BC

Pages 24-25 continued:

Votive barge
Thonis-Heracleion
4th–2nd century BC

Diver with perfume jar

Four colossal objects on board a boat (L-R):
Colossal statue of a Ptolemaic pharaoh
Stele of Ptolemy VIII, after 118 BC
Colossal statue of a Ptolemaic queen
Colossal statue of Hapy, 4th century BC
Thonis-Heracleion

Simpulum
Thonis-Heracleion
4th–2nd century BC

Sistrum
Origin unknown
332–30 BC

Raising Hapy

Diver with sphinx

Back cover:

Pages 28-29:

Diver with processional barge

Diver with boat

Statue of Egyptian priest with sphinxes

ACKNOWLEDGEMENTS

With special thanks to the team at the British Museum:
Aurelia Masson-Berghoff, Daniela Rosenow, Jane Batty, Jane Findlay and Emma Poulter.

We would like to thank Franck Goddio, Director of Excavations of Thonis-Heracleion and Canopus, and his colleagues, for their input.

We would also like to thank the Egyptian Ministry of Antiquities, and particularly the Egyptian Museum (Cairo), the Graeco-Roman Museum (Alexandria), the Maritime Museum (Alexandria), the National Museum (Alexandria) and the Bibliotheca Alexandrina Antiquities Museum (Alexandria).

PUBLISHER'S NOTE

This book was created for children, to educate but even more importantly to entertain. Although every attempt at factual accuracy has been made, it is not within the scope of this book to present an exhaustive, academic treatment of this fascinating subject. Any errors, ommissions or misinterpretations are ours, not those of the British Museum or its experts.

THIRD INTERMEDIATE PERIOD
1069–664 BC

900 BC

LATE PERIOD
664–332 BC

664–610 BC
Reign of Pharaoh Psamtik I, who hires Greek soldiers to help him free Egypt from Assyrian control.

Thonis-Heracleion becomes a major trading port on the Mediterranean Sea.

[…] to build their own […] in Naukratis.

600 BC

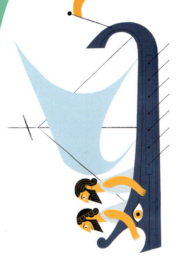

525–404 BC
The Persians control Egypt.

450 BC
Herodotus visits Thonis-Heracleion and Naukratis.

380 BC
Decree of Sais shows that customs duties were levied at Thonis-Heracleion and Naukratis.

343–332 BC
Persians conquer Egypt again. The Egyptians are not happy.

PTOLEMAIC PERIOD 332–30 BC

332 BC Alexander the Great arrives in Egypt and becomes its new ruler. He is very popular.

331 BC Alexander the Great founds a new city, Alexandria.

323 BC Alexander dies and Alexander's friend and general Ptolemy takes over.

305 BC Ptolemy I becomes pharaoh.

300 BC Greek becomes the official language of government but hieroglyphs are also used.

246–222 BC Ptolemy III builds temples to Serapis and Osiris.

196 BC The Rosetta Stone is carved.

51 BC Cleopatra VII becomes the last pharaoh of Egypt.

46 BC Cleopatra visits Rome, and promotes the cults of Serapis and Isis.

30 BC Roman Emperor Augustus takes control of Egypt. The Romans are interested in Egyptian culture and religion.

ROMAN PERIOD 30 BC–AD 641

1 AD

AD 391 Temples of Serapis are destroyed.

AD 700s Canopus and Thonis-Heracleion are completely submerged by the sea.

AD 2000 Canopus and Thonis-Heracleion are rediscovered!

THIS TIMELINE IS NOT TO SCALE!

WHAT HAPPENED WHEN

Our story starts around 664 BC, after a long period of war, when Egypt has been invaded several times...

THIRD INTERMEDIATE PERIOD 1069–664 BC

900 BC

664–610 BC
Reign of Pharaoh Psamtik I, who hires Greek soldiers to help him free Egypt from Assyrian control.

620–525 BC
Greek traders are allowed to build their own sanctuaries in Naukratis.

LATE PERIOD 664–332 BC

600 BC
Thonis-Heracleion becomes a major trading port on the Mediterranean Sea.

525–404 BC
The Persians control Egypt.

450 BC
Herodotus visits Thonis-Heracleion and Naukratis.

380 BC
Decree of Sais shows that customs duties were levied at Thonis-Heracleion and Naukratis.

343–332 BC
Persians conquer Egypt again. The Egyptians are not happy.

ONE WORLD

WELCOME TO EGYPT! TAXES, PLEASE!

THONIS-HERACLEION AND CANOPUS

ALEXANDRIA

SAIS

NAUKRATIS

MEMPHIS

EGYPT

River Nile

TWO PEOPLES,

GREECE

GOODBYE, GREEKS!

DELPHI

ATHENS

CORINTH

OLYMPIA

SPARTA

CRETE

SEA OF THE GREEKS
(or Mediterranean Sea)

PTOLEMAIC PERIOD 332–30 BC

331 BC Alexander the Great founds a new city, Alexandria.

332 BC Alexander the Great arrives in Egypt and becomes its new ruler. He is very popular.

323 BC Alexander dies and Alexander's friend and general Ptolemy takes over.

246–222 BC Ptolemy III builds temples to Serapis and Osiris.

300 BC

305 BC Ptolemy I becomes pharaoh.

Greek becomes the official language of government but hieroglyphs are also used.

196 BC The Rosetta Stone is carved.

51 BC Cleopatra VII becomes the last pharaoh of Egypt.

46 BC Cleopatra visits Rome, and promotes the cults of Serapis and Isis.

30 BC Roman Emperor Augustus takes control of Egypt. The Romans are interested in Egyptian culture and religion.

ROMAN PERIOD 30 BC – AD 641

1 AD

AD 391 Temples of Serapis are destroyed.

AD 700s Canopus and Thonis-Heracleion are completely submerged by the sea.

AD 2000 Canopus and Thonis-Heracleion are rediscovered!

THIS TIMELINE IS NOT TO SCALE!